Shadows

by Beverley Dietz

Someone is walking
down the street.
Do you see the shadow?
How big it is! Who could
have this big shadow?

It's me! I'm not big, but right now my shadow is. Later today, my shadow will get small—very small. Do you know why?

2

Look in the sky. Where is the sun?
How do our shadows look?
Let's wait awhile and then look at our
shadows again.

Where is the sun now? It's high in the
sky, right over our heads. Look at our
shadows now!

Look now! Our shadows
grew big again.
Where is the sun now?

You make shadows, too.
When the sun is out, you make a
shadow on the ground.
In the morning, your shadow is very
big because of where the sun is.

Later in the day, your shadow is very small.

Later on, your shadow gets big again.
Why? Because of the sun!

Let's have some fun. Look at these
shadows. What do you think
made them?

A house made
this shadow.

A horse made
this shadow.

This is a shadow
of a window.

And this is a shadow of a city!

Is the sun out today? Can you make shadows outside? If not, you can make shadows in your school room.

Do you know what animal this is?
How about this one?

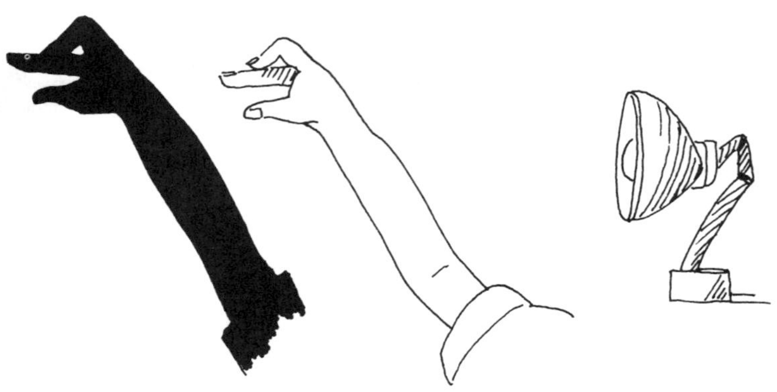

You can make these shadows, too!

10

Look at this shadow. It looks like a
bird trapped in someone's hand. But
it's a shadow made with three hands.

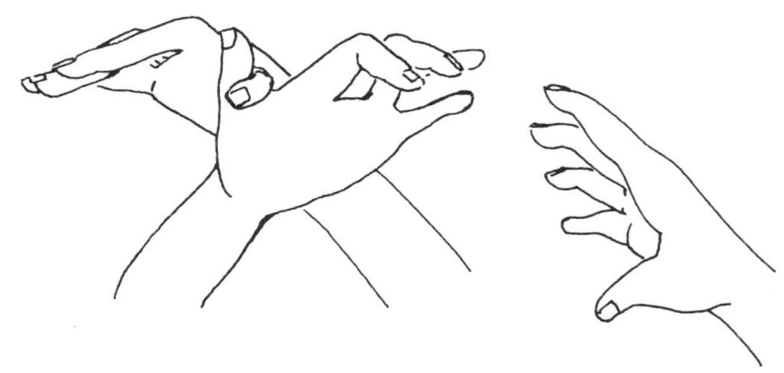

Here is some more shadow fun.
What shadows will you make?

All Smiles

Use with "Dreams."

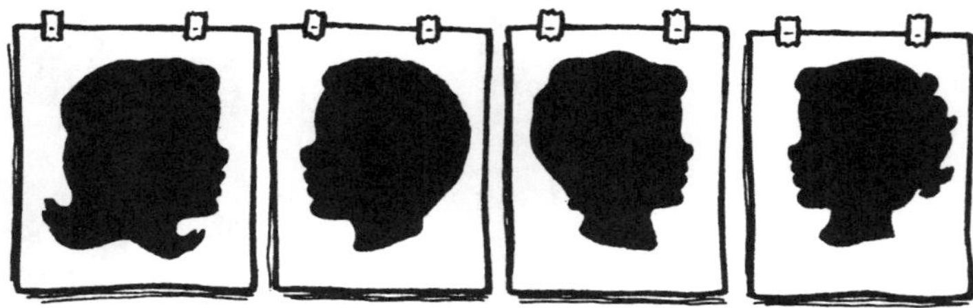